# GRAMMAR RAY
# ADJECTIVES

## a graphic guide to grammar
### andrew carter

Published by Evans Brothers Limited
2A Portman Mansions
Chiltern Street
London W1U 6NR

© in this edition Evans Brothers Limited 2010
© in the text and illustration Andrew Carter 2010

Printed in Malta by Gutenberg Press

Editor: Sophie Schrey
Designer: Mark Holt

British Library Cataloguing in Publication Data

Carter, Andrew.
Adjectives. — (Grammar Ray)
1. English language—Adjective—Juvenile literature.
I. Title II. Series
425.5-dc22

ISBN-13: 9780237538491

VISIT OUR WEBSITE
www.evansbooks.co.uk
Evans

# contents

# INTRODUCTION

Hello and welcome to Grammar Ray! You are about to enter a world of fun and adventure, where English grammar is brought to life. Words in the English language can be divided into different groups called 'parts of speech'. In this title, we will join the robots in their quest to explore the role of the adjective.

Hello! My name is Mr Adjective. I am on a mission to find the magician's missing wand.

The first part of the book is a comic strip. Join Mr Adjective on his adventure to solve the mystery of the missing magic wand and meet some interesting characters along the way! Look out for the words in red – they are key to the story.

After you've followed Mr Adjective's quest the rest of the book looks at adjectives in more detail, and gives some more examples. Use this if you need a reminder of the role adjectives play in English grammar. It also requires your puzzle-solving skills, and tests what you have learnt along the way. So be sure to pay attention!

# Let's revise nouns

Adjectives are words that can tell us more about nouns. Before we take a closer look, let's remind ourselves what we know about nouns.

Nouns are the words we use to name things. For example:

a stage,

a magician,

a hat,

a rabbit

a monkey,

some monkey

mischief,

panic.

# The Adjective

Saturday 16th March 3012    R 45

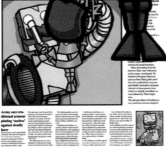

Adjectives are words that can tell us more about nouns.

A red robot was cleaning when a poster caught his eye.

Adjectives are often placed immediately in front of the noun they refer to, so they are easy to spot.

The robot had a brilliant idea...

...he used his special key to open the magician's secret room.

The magician's hat was on a tall table.

There was a bright light inside.

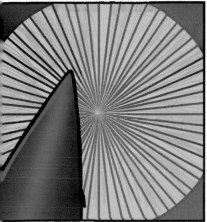  

The robot peered over the edge and fell into the deep hole...

...down a long tunnel...

...and landed on some soft, green grass.

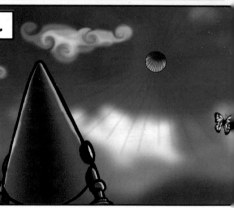

Adjectives can describe different things such as size, colour, emotion and nationality.

A small, white rabbit,

10

some happy rabbits.

Look!

The magic wand!

Words like 'very' and 'really' [ca]n be placed before adjectives to strengthen their meaning.

A *very* hard rock,

a *really* soft armchair,

a **very** tasty feast.

Adjectives can also be used to compare two or more nouns. For example:

a big carrot,

a bigger carrot,

the biggest carrot.

The magic wand turned them into a huge pile of carrot pieces.

The hungry rabbits approached,

followed by...

...a big, mean hare.

By adding a hyphen (-) to certain words in a sentence, we can create compound adjectives.
For example:
a 'hare eating carrot'
(noun)    (verb)    (noun)

could become...

a hare-eating carrot.
(compound adjective)  (noun)

A kind-hearted rabbit helped the carrot-eating hare.

14

Clever rabbits...

...what a good idea!

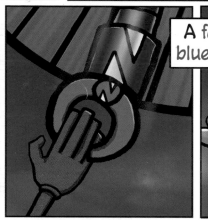

A familiar,
blue hand...

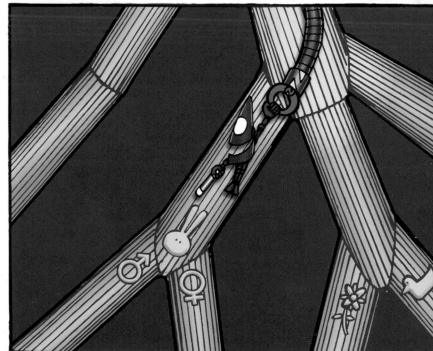

...a wonderful surprise.

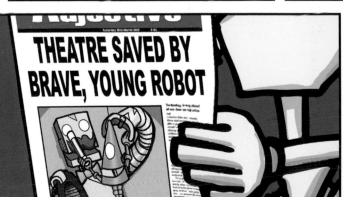

THEATRE SAVED BY BRAVE, YOUNG ROBOT

The end

## Adjectives

An adjective is a word that tells us more about a noun.
We can spot adjectives in a sentence quite easily as they are often placed immediately in front of the noun they refer to.

FOR EXAMPLE:     *the <u>red</u> robot, a <u>large</u> carrot, <u>funny</u> people*

**There are several types of adjective.**

**DESCRIPTIVE ADJECTIVES**

Descriptive adjectives are the most common type of adjective. They describe the quality, state or action of things and can tell us about size, colour, shape, emotional state and nationality.

FOR EXAMPLE:     *a <u>large</u> dinosaur, a <u>small</u> house, a <u>giant</u> spider*

*a <u>purple</u> flower, a <u>green</u> tomato, a <u>yellow</u> car*

*a <u>round</u> table, a <u>square</u> mirror, a <u>thin</u> boy*

*<u>happy</u> people, an <u>angry</u> rabbit, the <u>crazy</u> monkey*

*a <u>Japanese</u> fish, an <u>English</u> rose, an <u>African</u> zebra.*

**NUMERICAL ADJECTIVES**

Numerical adjectives can show the number or order of things.

FOR EXAMPLE:     **NUMBER:**
*<u>one</u> horse, <u>twenty</u> soldiers,*
*<u>one hundred</u> sweets, <u>each</u> person*

**INDEFINITE NUMBER:**
*<u>many</u> tigers, <u>several</u> mice,*
*<u>some</u> grass, a <u>few</u> options*

**ORDER:**
*<u>first</u> place, <u>second</u> in command, <u>final</u> bell*

# comparing adjectives

Adjectives can be used to compare nouns.
Adjectives have three levels of comparison called the positive,
comparative and superlative.

FOR EXAMPLE:

a _big_ carrot
(POSITIVE)

a _bigger_ carrot
(COMPARATIVE)

the _biggest_ carrot
(SUPERLATIVE)

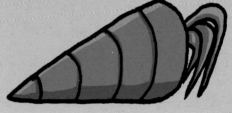

**Let's look in a bit more detail.**

**POSITIVE**

The positive shows the basic form of the adjective.

FOR EXAMPLE:

_a _hot_ country, a _wise_ man, an _important_ exam_

**COMPARATIVE**

The comparative shows that the noun has more of the adjective quality than just the basic, or positive adjective. We use the comparative when we are comparing two things. To create a comparative we usually add  _–er_ to the end of the adjective. However this doesn't always work and you will be able to tell if the ending sounds wrong. For longer adjectives, for example, we use '_more_' before the word.

FOR EXAMPLE:

_England was _hot_, but Spain was _hotter_._
_He thought he was _wise_, but his sister was _wiser_._
_The other exam was _more important_._

## SUPERLATIVE

The superlative shows when the noun has the maximum amount of the adjective quality, above the level of the others. We use the superlative when we compare three or more things. To create a superlative we usually add −*est* to the end of the adjective. But, as with comparative adjectives, this doesn't always work. For longer adjectives in the superlative we use '*most*' before the word.

**NOTE:**

We use the article '*the*' when using the superlative.

**FOR EXAMPLE:**

*Egypt was <u>the hottest</u> country.*
*He was <u>the wisest</u> of the three men.*
*This exam is <u>the most important</u>.*

Some adjectives have irregular comparative and superlative forms.

**FOR EXAMPLE:**

*good, better, best*
*many, more, most*
*bad, worse, worst*
*little, less, least*

# compound adjectives

**A compound adjective is formed when two or more adjectives work together to describe the noun. They are joined by a hyphen (-).**

FOR EXAMPLE:

*long-lasting, paper-thin, mouth-watering*

By adding a hyphen we can greatly change the meaning of sentence: compound adjectives often mean something completely different to the original words they are formed from.

**Let's look again at the example from the comic:**

FOR EXAMPLE:

| a hare | eating | carrot | = | a hare eating some carrot |
|--------|--------|--------|---|---------------------------|
| (NOUN) | (VERB) | (NOUN) | | |

| a | hare-eating | carrot | = | a carrot that eats hares |
|---|-------------|--------|---|--------------------------|
| | (COMPOUND) ADJECTIVE | (NOUN) | | |

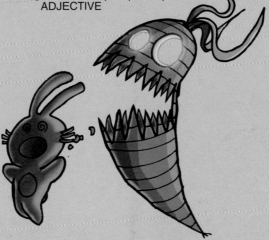

# adjectives
## test yourself

**1. Which two words in the following list are *not* adjectives?**

lucky, orange, in, Dutch, smooth, run, few

**2. Choose the adjectives to complete the sentence.***

A ------, ------ robot with
---, -------, ---- arms.

hot   red   big   lazy
yellow   round   triangular
square   blue   many

*\* HINT: The dashes show the number of letter spaces available.*

**3. Match the following words and pictures:**
**(a) four armed robots**
**(b) four-armed robots**

1.

2.

Turn the page upside-down to see the answers!

(1) in, run (2) A round, yellow robot with big, square, blue arms. (3) 1-a, 2-b

# INDEX

# enjoy more of the wonderful world of

# Grammar Ray

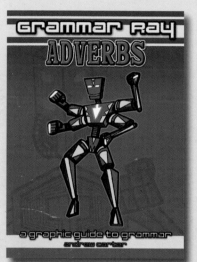

Grammar Ray
ADVERBS
a graphic guide to grammar
andrew carter

ISBN: 9780237538507

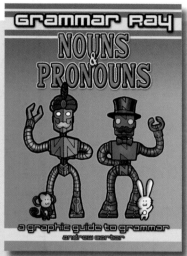

Grammar Ray
NOUNS & PRONOUNS
a graphic guide to grammar
andrew carter

ISBN: 9780237537685

Grammar Ray
PREPOSITIONS
a graphic guide to grammar
andrew carter

ISBN: 9780237538514

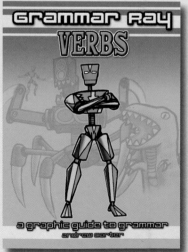

Grammar Ray
VERBS
a graphic guide to grammar
andrew carter

ISBN: 9780237538484

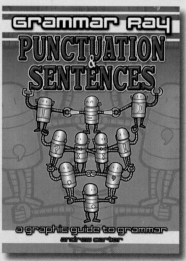

Grammar Ray
PUNCTUATION & SENTENCES
a graphic guide to grammar
andrew carter

ISBN: 9780237538521